clay pot

cooking

clay pot

cooking

Elsa Petersen-Schepelern | *photography by* **Gus Filgate**

TIME LIFE BOOKS

Alexandria, Virginia

TIME® LIFE BOOKS

Time-Life Books is a division of Time Life Inc.

TIME LIFE INC.

President and CEO: George Artandi

TIME-LIFE CUSTOM PUBLISHING

Vice President and Publisher   Terry Newell
Vice President of Sales and Marketing   Neil Levin
Director of Acquisitions   Jennifer Pearce
Director of Creative Services   Laura Ciccone McNeill
Director of Special Markets   Liz Ziehl
Project Manager   Jennie Halfant

TIME-LIFE is a trademark of Time Warner Inc. U.S.A.
Books produced by Time-Life Custom Publishing are available at a special
bulk discount for promotional and premium use. Custom adaptations can
also be created to meet your specific marketing goals. Call 1-800-323-5255.

Petersen-Schepelern, Elsa
  Clay pot cooking : from tandoori to tagine / Elsa Petersen-Schepelern :
  with photography by Gus Filgate
      p. cm.
  ISBN 0-7370-2017-2
  1. Clay pot cookery. 2. Cookery. International. I. Title.
TX825.5.P48 1999
641.5'89--dc21   99-28216
                                    CIP

First published in the United Kingdom in 1999 by
Ryland Peters & Small, 51–55 Mortimer Street, London W1N 7TD.
Text copyright © Elsa Petersen-Schepelern 1999.
Design and illustrations copyright © Ryland Peters & Small 1999.

Printed and bound in China by Toppan Printing Co.

Publishing Director   Anne Ryland
Head of Design   Gabriella Le Grazie
Designer   Lucy Hamilton
Food Editor   Elsa Petersen-Schepelern
Production   Patricia Harrington
Food Stylist   Annie Nichols
Stylist   Penny Markham
Author Photograph   Francis Loney

Acknowledgments

My thanks to The Kasbah, Jerry's Home Store, Habitat, David Mellor, and
Heals in London for their help, and to Reco Ltd for permission to use the
Romertopf® trademark. Thanks also to Kirsten and Peter Bray, Anders Ous-
back, Imtiaz Quereshi, Veronica Valentina-Capezza, Janet Cato, Luc Vo Tan,
Robert Roseman, Barbara Beckett, Richard Deutsh, Sheridan Lear, and Tim.

Notes

All spoon measurements are level unless otherwise noted.
Raw or partly cooked eggs should not be served to the very young,
the old, the frail, or to pregnant women.
Specialty Asian ingredients are available in large supermarkets,
Thai, Chinese, Japanese and Vietnamese stores, as well as Asian stores.

contents

cooking
in
clay pots

Traditional clay cooking pots are used all over the world: Moroccans use the tagine with its conical lid, the Spanish a lidless cazuela, and in Provence, the shallow open dish called a tian is also the dish cooked in it. Other vessels, of earthenware or stoneware, include chicken bricks, tandoor pots, potato or bean pots, garlic or onion bakers, soufflé dishes, pie dishes, glazed ceramic casseroles, and Chinese sand pots—all great ways to cook many kinds of food, but especially good for slow-cooked dishes.

Follow the manufacturer's advice on the correct cooking method for each vessel, but a general guide is that unglazed earthenware, such as terra cotta, should be soaked in cold water for about 10–20 minutes before use, and should never be washed in detergent or in a dishwasher, which will taint the clay. Chicken bricks and Romertopfs® are perhaps the best examples of such vessels. Don't use them for very highly flavored dishes, such as curries or fish dishes, in case they absorb the flavors and taint other dishes. Glazed earthenware such as the cazuela and the tagine should never be placed in or on the heat while empty, and all earthenware should be placed in a cold oven, then brought up to the correct heat (gradually, in stages if it is a gas oven).

Some clay pots were traditionally used on top of the stove, but you should follow the manufacturer's instructions, and it would be wise to use a heat diffuser between the heat source and the pot. I myself would always prefer to use them in the oven rather than on top of the stove. Moroccan tagines, however, can also be used on a barbecue, though the coals should be covered with sand.

Stoneware is a stronger material, fired at 2307°F, and usually glazed—much ceramic ovenware is of this kind and can be placed in a preheated oven without fear of damage, but always check the manufacturer's instructions. Never put a hot pot on a cold surface.

The dishes in this book have been created with clay pot cooking in mind, but they can be adapted for cast iron or stainless steel by placing the metal pots in a preheated oven and reducing the cooking times accordingly—usually about 30 minutes.

An important point—all dishes containing liquid should be brought to a boil at a high heat first, then reduced to a simmer. The time it takes to reach that high heat will vary between ovens, so it is impossible to give precise times.

This is a healthier, more modern, New World version of a traditional hearty Swedish soup—and there are even some Swedes who prefer it! In the original recipe, the peas are cooked with salt pork or ham, which is shredded into the soup before serving. If you soak the peas for 30 minutes before cooking, this dish is even faster.

Swedish Yellow Pea Soup
with Crispy Bacon, Sour Cream, and Herbs

Place the first 7 ingredients in a glazed bean pot or other clay casserole dish, put in a cold oven, turn to 400°F, and bring to a boil. Reduce to 300°F and cook for about 20 minutes. Test the peas—they should be whole, but soft. If not, cook for 5–10 minutes more—the time will depend on the age of the peas.

Remove the cloves, bay leaves, and orange zest, and serve the peas immediately or, for a smoother texture, purée in a blender or food processor, in batches if necessary. Stir in the mustard and season to taste. (If you prefer a brighter color, remove the carrot and onions before blending.) Meanwhile, cut the bacon into strips and sauté until crisp. Serve the soup topped with crispy bacon, a tablespoon of sour cream, and snipped chives or parsley.

2 cups dried yellow split peas
4 cups hot ham or pork stock
2 onions, *halved lengthwise*
1 carrot, *thickly sliced*
6 cloves, *stuck in the onions*
3 fresh bay leaves
3 long curls of orange zest
4 tablespoons Dijon mustard
salt and freshly ground pepper

To Serve

4 slices smoked bacon or 8 very thin slices smoked pancetta
¼ cup sour cream
snipped chives, or parsley

serves 4

Soups and appetizers

Whatever you do, don't salt beans until they have finished their first cooking. Salt a bean beforehand and you can cook it all day and it will still stay hard! You can also leave the beans whole, drain, then toss in salt and olive oil, and serve with roast lamb. Other small dried beans are also good. Serve with toasted ciabatta bread.

Italian Bean Soup
with Rosemary and Garlic

1¼ cups dried cannellini beans

1 onion, *sliced*

1 carrot, *quartered*

1 large sprig of rosemary

4 garlic cloves, *lightly crushed*

½ cup olive oil

1 large onion, *sliced*

1 fresh red chili, *cored, seeded, and sliced*

6 garlic cloves, *4 crushed, 2 sliced*

2 tomatoes, *skinned, seeded, and chopped*

3 waxy potatoes, such as Yukon Gold, *coarsely diced, then rinsed*

2 carrots, *coarsely diced*

2 celery stalks, *finely diced*

12 oz. Savoy cabbage, *finely sliced*

2 sprigs of rosemary

salt and freshly ground black pepper

serves 4

To cook the beans, first soak them overnight in cold water to cover. Drain, rinse, and place in a bean pot with the onion, carrot, rosemary, and garlic. Cover with water, put in a cold oven, turn to 400°F, and bring to a boil. Reduce to a simmer and cook gently until done (the time will depend on the age of the beans). Drain the liquid into a measuring pitcher and make up to 4 cups with boiling water. Tip the beans into a bowl, then remove and discard the vegetables and flavorings. Sprinkle the beans with salt and purée half in a food processor, then transfer all the beans back into the clay pot.

Heat 6 tablespoons of the oil in a skillet, add the onion and chili, sprinkle with salt, and sauté until the onion is soft and translucent. Add the crushed garlic and cook until golden. Transfer to the pot with the tomatoes, vegetables, rosemary, and liquid and bring to a boil in the hot oven. Reduce to 350°F and simmer for 30 minutes. Season to taste. Heat the remaining oil in a skillet and sauté the sliced garlic until golden. Discard the rosemary, ladle the soup into heated bowls, top with the golden sautéed garlic, and serve with toasted ciabatta.

One of my favorite chefs in all the world is Anders Ousback, who helped make living in Sydney, Australia, one of the great gastronomic experiences. One of his best summer dishes was baked garlic with goat cheese, toast, and arugula. Try this version with Greek feta or broiled cheese and a peppery salad—I love it with nasturtium leaves and flowers. Press the nutty-flavored garlic flesh out of each clove, then spread it on the cheese.

Oven-roasted Garlic
with Cheese and Leaves

Either leave the garlic heads whole or cut a "lid" off the top, brush with olive oil and sprinkle with a little salt (optional, but it helps the garlic soften quicker). Place the heads of garlic in a garlic baker or small glazed clay baking dish, put in a cold oven, and cook at 400°F for 40 minutes, or until the cloves are soft and creamy. Just before serving, mix the vinaigrette ingredients (take care adding salt, because feta and haloumi cheese can be very salty). Place a tangle of leaves on each salad plate. Add the sliced feta cheese to the plates. If you like, you can sauté the slices briefly on each side in a lightly oiled preheated skillet. Add the pine nuts to the skillet and shake the skillet a few times. When the nuts are golden (about 30 seconds), sprinkle over the salads. Add the baked garlic and nasturtium flowers, if using, then sprinkle with the vinaigrette (or spray from a hand-held sprayer) and serve.

4 large whole heads of garlic

olive oil (see method)

mixed salad leaves, *including baby red chard, arugula, watercress, dandelion leaves, and nasturtium leaves*

about 8 oz. feta cheese, *cut into ¼-inch slices with a sharp knife*

2 tablespoons pine nuts

nasturtium flowers (if available)

Mild Japanese Vinaigrette

1 tablespoon Japanese white rice vinegar

6 tablespoons extra-virgin olive oil

lots of freshly ground black pepper

sea salt, to taste

serves 4

A Middle Eastern classic, usually made with little birds such as quail or poussins. It is easier if made with chicken thighs (you can bone them if you like, though the bone gives them more flavor). Omit the chicken if you'd prefer to make this a vegetarian dish. Double the quantities if you have very hungry guests, or if you want to serve this as a main course.

Stuffed Eggplants
on Spicy Harissa Couscous

4 medium eggplants, *peeled in strips (optional), and halved lengthwise*

4 chicken thighs (optional)

4 tablespoons olive oil

2 onions, *sliced*

3 garlic cloves, *crushed*

6 ripe red plum tomatoes, *skinned, seeded, and chopped*

salt and freshly ground black pepper

snipped fresh chives, to serve

Spicy Tunisian Harissa Couscous

1 lb. easy-cook couscous

2 cups boiling chicken or vegetable stock

2 teaspoons harissa paste

1 tablespoon butter

2 tablespoons snipped fresh chives

serves 4

Cut hollows in the cut surfaces of each eggplant. Sprinkle with salt and leave for 30 minutes. Rinse, pat dry, and char-grill or sauté on all sides until lightly browned. Set aside. Chop the cut-out flesh and reserve. Char-grill or sauté the chicken, if using, until lightly browned.

Heat the olive oil in a large skillet, add the onions, and sauté until translucent. Add the garlic and sauté for 1 minute. Add the tomatoes and reserved eggplant, bring to a boil, and simmer until thickened.

Place a few spoonfuls of the mixture in the base of a lidded clay pot and arrange 4 eggplant halves, cut-side up, on top. Place a spoonful of the mixture in each cavity, with a piece of chicken, if using, on top. Add another spoonful of sauce and place the remaining eggplant halves on top. Spoon the remaining sauce around and season to taste. Cover and roast at 400°F for 1 hour, or until the chicken is done.

Place the couscous in an ovenproof dish, pour over the stock, and put in the oven for the last 5 minutes of cooking. Drain if necessary, fork through the harissa, butter, and chives. Put 1–2 spoonfuls on each appetizer plate, add the eggplants and sauce, and sprinkle with extra chives.

Fish and seafood

Indian Coconut Fish Curry

Goa is the former Portuguese colony on the west coast of India. It mixes the cooking traditions of both countries in some of the world's most exciting fish dishes. This ginger-chili marinade gives wonderful flavor to the most ordinary fish varieties. Vegetable oil or ghee would be the usual cooking medium on the west coast of India—but if you can find mustard oil in an Asian food store, use that instead for an east-coast flavor. Use glazed clay pots for fish and other strong-tasting foods.

4 tablespoons chili oil

4 tablespoons ginger purée

2 teaspoons crushed fennel seeds

4 thick fish fillets, such as cod or halibut,
cut in half crosswise

2 teaspoons ground turmeric

2 tablespoons vegetable oil or mustard oil

1 tablespoon mustard seeds (optional)

2 onions, *halved and sliced lengthwise,
then separated into petals*

about 2 cups coconut milk, *heated*

2 red chilies, *seeded and sliced*

salt and freshly ground black pepper

sprigs of fresh cilantro, to serve

serves 4

To make the marinade, mix the chili oil, ginger, and crushed fennel seeds in a shallow dish. Rub the fish with the turmeric, then place in the chili oil mixture. Set aside for 2 hours or overnight. Heat the oil in a skillet, add the mustard seeds, if using, and cook until they pop. Add the onions and cook until golden. Add the fish (reserving the marinade) and cook at a high heat for 2 minutes until golden. Season to taste. Add the coconut milk, the remaining marinade, and the sliced red chilies. Bring to a boil, then transfer to a warmed, glazed clay pot. Simmer in a preheated oven at 450°F for 5–10 minutes until the fish is done. Serve with sprigs of cilantro and Indian accompaniments such as basmati rice and pappadams.

I first had the cold salad version of this dish in a restaurant on the edge of the Piazza in Siena—introduced to it by my 10-year-old Italian cousin. This is a hot version, using fresh tuna rather than the traditional canned fish. I think it's better! White cannellini beans are usual for this dish, but I like the taste and pretty green color of French flageolets if you can find them. It's the perfect way to use up beans cooked for another dish. This is enough for an appetizer, or for a main course for lunch, with lots of green salad and freshly baked crusty bread. Tuna can be expensive, so this recipe is a good way of making one wonderful steak stretch a little further.

Tonno e Fagioli al Forno

4 tablespoons olive oil

2 onions, *finely sliced*

3 fat garlic cloves, *crushed*

2 lbs. cooked or canned green flageolet beans or white cannellini beans, or a mixture of both

sea salt and freshly ground black pepper

1 large tuna steak, about 8 oz.

To Serve

¼ cup sliced fresh basil, plus lots of extra sprigs

serves 4

Heat half of the oil in a skillet, add the sliced onions and cook gently until softened and translucent. Add the garlic, stir well, and cook for about 1 minute until golden. Add the beans, stir well, add salt and freshly ground black pepper to taste, then heat until sizzling.

Place half the beans in a lidded glazed clay pot, place the tuna on top, then spoon in the remaining bean mixture. Sprinkle with the remaining oil, cover with a lid, and cook in the oven at 400°F for about 20 minutes. Remove and test the fish: it should be moist, but flake easily. If not, cook for a few minutes more, then remove from the pot and discard the skin and central bone. Stir in the sliced basil.

Divide the beans and tuna between 4 heated bowls and sprinkle with sprigs of basil. Serve with crusty bread and Italian red wine.

This is the quickest, easiest bouillabaisse ever. Not as grand as the real thing on the beach in the south of France, but much easier to cope with! Personally, I think the fish is much nicer cooked this way, because it hasn't had all the texture and flavor boiled out of it. Add the shrimp and scallops at the very end—they will firm up in the boiling stock. The squid, in particular, is gorgeous like this. Use firm fish like cod or shark as the white fish, as well as a red fish like snapper (red fish always tastes wonderful). About 2 lbs. mussels could also be added to this dish at the end—steam them open first with a cupful of white wine in a pan on top of the stove.

Bouillabaisse

To make the rouille, purée the egg yolk, garlic, chili and tomato pastes in a blender or food processor until smooth. Add the olive oil, a little at a time, as if making mayonnaise. When very thick, blend in the lemon juice, season to taste, and transfer to a small bowl.

Heat the oil in a skillet, cook the onions until translucent and golden, add the garlic, and cook for 1 minute more. Transfer to a heated, glazed lidded casserole, add the boiling stock, wine, saffron, and seasoning, and cook in the oven at 400°F until it has boiled for about 10 minutes. Add the white and red fish and squid, and return just to boiling point. Add the shrimp and scallops, put the lid back on the pot and bring to the table. Serve with the toasted baguette and rouille.

Rouille

1 egg yolk

1 garlic clove, *crushed*

1 teaspoon hot red chili paste

1 tablespoon sun-dried tomato paste

1 cup olive oil

1 tablespoon lemon juice

sea salt

2 tablespoons olive oil

2 large onions, *finely sliced*

4–6 garlic cloves, *crushed*

4 cups boiling fish stock

½ cup white wine

2 pinches of saffron threads, *soaked in boiling water for 30 minutes (or 2 sachets of saffron powder)*

salt and freshly ground black pepper

8 oz. boneless white fish fillets, such as cod or halibut

8 oz. boneless red fish fillets, such as red snapper

8 oz. prepared baby squid (optional)

1 lb. uncooked shrimp, *shelled and deveined*

8 scallops, *halved crosswise if large*

sliced baguette, *rubbed with garlic and olive oil, then toasted,* to serve

serves 4

Poultry and

game

Moroccan Spiced Chicken

with Preserved Lemons

An easy, modern version of a traditional Moroccan dish. Serve with plain couscous or Chickpea Tagine with Spring Vegetables on page 54. I like the preserved lemon cooked with the chicken from the beginning, rather than added at the very end in the usual way. I also like this recipe without the olives, though they are traditional. Ginger is not usual in this dish either, but I think it adds immeasurably to the verve of the recipe.

1 free-range, corn-fed chicken

4 garlic cloves, *cut into fine slivers*

1 inch fresh root ginger, *cut into fine slivers*

2 tablespoons olive oil

2 large onions, *grated*

2 pinches of saffron strands, *soaked in boiling water for 30 minutes (or 2 sachets saffron powder)*

2 cinnamon sticks

sliced peel of 1 preserved lemon (make your own, or buy from Middle Eastern food stores)*

12 small black olives (optional)

salt and freshly ground black pepper

sprigs of cilantro

easy-cook couscous, to serve

serves 4

Make small slits in the breast of the chicken and insert the slivers of garlic and ginger. Heat the oil in a skillet and sauté the chicken on all sides until golden. Transfer to a tagine or other clay pot. Add the grated onions, saffron, cinnamon sticks, and sliced preserved lemon peel. Add 1 cup water, cover, place in a cold oven, turn to 450°, and bring to a boil. Reduce to 300° and simmer for 1½–2 hours, or until the chicken is done. Stir in the olives, if using, season to taste, add the cilantro, and serve with couscous.

To make preserved lemons, cut fruit into quarters, leaving attached at the stem end. Put 1 tablespoon salt in each and put in a preserving jar with cloves, cinnamon sticks, and fresh bay leaves. Add 6 tablespoons salt, juice of 2 lemons, and top up with boiling water. Seal and use after 2 weeks.

In India, a tandoor is a huge clay oven used to cook kabobs, fish, meat, poultry, and breads. Smaller tandoor clay pots are now available in the West, and you can also use a broiler. Ajwain or ajowan is a spice found in Asian food stores, but if you can't find it, use fennel seeds instead. A lurid red food coloring is also added in some restaurants, but many of the top Indian chefs prefer the more subtle natural color of the spices.

Tandoori Chicken

Tandoori Paste

2 tablespoons vegetable oil

2 teaspoons mustard seeds

2 teaspoons coriander seeds

2 teaspoons ajwain or fennel seeds

1 teaspoon red chili flakes

1 teaspoon ground turmeric

1 tablespoon grated fresh ginger

1 tablespoon fresh garlic purée

2 tablespoons sesame oil

4–5 tablespoons plain yogurt

3 tablespoons heavy cream

2 tablespoons lemon or lime juice

2 tablespoons chopped fresh cilantro

salt and freshly ground black pepper

2 lbs. chicken breast, *cut into thin strips*

lime wedges, cilantro, and salad, to serve

serves 4

To make the tandoori paste, heat half the oil in a skillet, add the mustard seeds, and heat until they pop. Add the coriander seeds, ajwain or fennel seeds, chili, turmeric, salt, and pepper and stir-fry for 1 minute until aromatic. Add the ginger and garlic and stir-fry until the garlic is golden. Put the remaining paste ingredients in a food processor and add the fried aromatics. Blend until smooth.

Thread the chicken onto steel or soaked bamboo skewers and place in a shallow dish. Cover with the tandoori paste, turning the skewers until the chicken is well coated. Chill for at least 30 minutes.

When ready to cook, prepare the tandoor pot according to the manufacturer's instructions. Add the skewers and cook for about 8 minutes or according to the manufacturer's instructions. Baste with the remaining oil and cook for 2 minutes more, or until the chicken is done. Alternatively, if using a broiler, oil the broiler pan first. Add the skewers and cook for about 5 minutes until crispy on one side, then turn them over and cook for 3 minutes on the other side. Serve with lemon or lime wedges, sprigs of cilantro, and mixed peppery leaves.

A classic French recipe given a modern twist. Traditionally, the cavity of the chicken would be filled with this herby dressing, but this isn't recommended these days. Instead, you could fill the neck end before trussing the chicken, and then tie the remaining dressing in muslin as below.

Poule au Pot

To make the dressing, put the bread in a bowl. Moisten with milk, then squeeze out the excess milk and return the bread to the rinsed bowl. Heat the oil in a skillet and cook the bacon, if using, until crispy. Add to the breadcrumbs. Sauté the onion until translucent, add the garlic, sauté for 1 minute, then add to the bowl. Mix in the tarragon and egg. Fill the neck of the chicken with the dressing and tie up the remainder in muslin.

Heat the olive oil in the skillet and brown the chicken on all sides. Transfer to a glazed clay pot. Brown the large vegetables and garlic and add to the pot. Deglaze the skillet with the wine, stir up the brown bits, and pour into the pot. Tie up the cabbage with string and tuck in beside the bird, together with the herbs. Season then cover with stock. Place in a cold oven and turn to 450°F until the stock boils, then reduce to a bare simmer and cook for 1½–2 hours or until very tender. After 1–1¼ hours, brown the small onions or shallots in the skillet, add to the pot with the other small vegetables and the dressing, and cook until tender.

To serve, place the chicken on a large serving plate, and surround with the small poached vegetables, the unwrapped dressing, and the cabbage. Discard the large vegetables and strain the pot juices into a small pitcher. Serve with new potatoes, the juices, and homemade aïoli or mayonnaise.

Tarragon Dressing

6 slices stale bread, *torn, crusts removed*

½ cup milk

1 tablespoon olive oil

4 slices smoked bacon or pancetta

(optional), *scissor-snipped*

1 onion, *finely diced*

2 garlic cloves, *crushed*

1 tablespoon chopped fresh tarragon leaves

1 beaten egg

4 tablespoons olive oil or butter

1 whole chicken

2 large onions, *quartered*,

and 12 small onions or shallots

1 large carrot, *sliced*, and 6 small carrots

1 large parsnip, *thickly sliced*,

and 6 small parsnips

1 large turnip, *sliced*, and 6 baby turnips

6 garlic cloves

1 cup white wine

1 small cabbage, such as Savoy

1 bundle of fresh herbs (bouquet garni)

salt and freshly ground black pepper

2 cups chicken stock

serves 4

A tremendously easy recipe, packed with spicy flavors. Thai shops have a wonderful variety of eggplants—tiny pea-sized ones, gooseberry-sized ones with green and purple stripes, egg-sized ones in pale green, white, or bright yellow—even long pale green ones like zucchinis. If you can't find these more esoteric varieties, use small Chinese or Japanese eggplants and cut them in half lengthwise—or even 1 large purple one, diced.

Thai Chicken
with Eggplants in Coconut Milk

Spicy Marinade

2 tablespoons puréed or grated ginger

6 garlic cloves, *crushed*

1 teaspoon ground turmeric

2 tablespoons chili oil

2 tablespoons Thai fish sauce

2 tablespoons light soy sauce

Mix the marinade ingredients in a flat dish, add the chicken pieces, and turn to coat well. Cover and marinate in the refrigerator for 30 minutes or overnight.

When ready to cook, heat the corn and chili oils in a wok or skillet. Add the cinnamon sticks, ginger, and garlic, and sauté for 1 minute. Add the chicken and sauté until browned.

Place the shallots in a small bowl, cover with boiling water, then slip off the skins. If using large ones, separate the two lobes. Add to the skillet and sauté with the chicken.

Add the marinade, all the eggplants, the kaffir lime leaves, if using, the lime zest, lemongrass, chilies, and coconut milk and heat gently.

Transfer to a Chinese sand pot or shallow, glazed, lidded clay pot. Place in a cold oven and turn to 450°F until the contents come to a boil. Immediately reduce to a gentle simmer and cook for 45 minutes, or until the chicken is done. Serve with fragrant Thai rice.

8–12 chicken thighs

2 tablespoons corn oil

1 tablespoon chili oil

2 cinnamon sticks

1 tablespoon puréed or grated ginger

6 garlic cloves, whole

6 shallots (or 24 small Thai shallots)

about 1 lb. eggplants (see introduction)

6 kaffir lime leaves, *sliced* (optional)

grated zest of 2 kaffir limes or 1 lime

2 stalks of lemongrass, *halved lengthwise and bruised with a mallet*

2 red Thai chilies, *seeded and sliced*

2 cups coconut milk

steamed fragrant Thai rice, to serve

serves 4

Dum Pukht is a cooking style from North India—*dum* means "steamed." I first tasted this style of cooking at the Delhi Sheraton, cooked by Imtiaz Quereshi, one of the finest chefs in India and the master of the Dum Pukht style. You can adapt this recipe for lamb, turkey, or other meats. When the dish is cooked, Imtiaz adds a lid of puff pastry and bakes until golden. The pastry is cut open at the table—it looks dramatic and smells marvelous!

Chicken Dum Pukht

2 tablespoons vegetable oil

2 tablespoons grated ginger

6 garlic cloves, *crushed*

1 tablespoon red Thai chili paste

2 sachets of saffron powder, a large pinch of saffron threads, or 2 teaspoons turmeric

1 tablespoon garam masala

1 whole chicken, *skinned and cut into pieces*

1 cup yogurt

½ cup heavy cream or sour cream

juice of 1 lemon

2 onions, *cut into wedges and separated into petals*

2 tomatoes, *skinned, quartered, and seeded*

1 red bell pepper, *peeled with a vegetable peeler, cored, seeded, and diced*

about 1 cup shelled green peas

serves 4

Heat half the oil in a skillet, add the ginger, garlic, chili paste, saffron, and garam masala, and stir-fry for a few minutes until the spices become aromatic. Transfer to a large shallow dish.

Make long cuts in the chicken, down to the bone, add to the dish and turn until well-coated with the spices. Rub the spices into the cuts. Add the yogurt, cream, and lemon juice, stir well and set aside to marinate for about 30 minutes.

Heat the remaining oil in a skillet, add the onions, and cook until softened and brown at the edges. Transfer the chicken mixture to a glazed clay pot, stir in the contents of the skillet, the tomatoes and red bell pepper, cover tightly with foil and a lid, and cook at 400°F until just below boiling (if yogurt boils it will separate). Reduce the heat to a simmer and continue cooking for 20 minutes. Add the peas, cover, and cook until the chicken is done, about 15 minutes.

Serve with other Indian dishes, such as the Spiced Chickpeas on page 57, steamed basmati rice, and naan bread.

Turkey is a low-fat, healthy meat—delicious slow-cooked in a covered clay pot with lots of assertive Mediterranean flavorings. Use a small whole breast or the thigh, which is packed with flavor and will serve four people (or two if they're very hungry). If you prefer, you can omit the bacon and brush the joint with a little soy sauce instead.

Turkey Pot-Roast
with Garlic, Pancetta, and Rosemary

Make slits all over the top of the turkey and insert slivers of garlic and very small sprigs of rosemary. Wrap the joint in pancetta or bacon. Heat the oil in a skillet, add the onions, and cook until translucent. Add the crushed garlic and sauté for 2 minutes more.

Place a layer of onions and garlic in the base of a soaked Romertopf® or other clay pot, then add the bay leaves and 2 large sprigs of rosemary.

Place the turkey on top and brush with olive oil. Pour in the wine or stock, sprinkle with pepper, place in a cold oven, turn to 400°F, and cook for about 1½ hours or until the turkey is cooked (the time will depend on the size of the joint). To test if the turkey is done, pierce the thickest part of the joint with a skewer—the juices should flow clear, with no trace of pink. If not, return to the oven and cook further.

Serve with one of the vegetable dishes in this book, or potatoes mashed with sun-dried tomatoes, char-grilled vegetables, and a leafy green salad.

1 turkey thigh or breast

9 garlic cloves, 3 *finely sliced, 6 crushed*

8 very small tip-sprigs of rosemary and 2 large sprigs

4–6 slices of pancetta or smoked bacon

2 tablespoons olive oil

3 red onions, *sliced*

2 fresh bay leaves

1 cup white wine or chicken stock

lots of freshly ground black pepper

serves 4

Chicken bricks are wonderful, but game birds in particular benefit from this gentle cooking method that prevents them from drying out. They are equally good served hot or cold (they make a glamorous picnic). Use a larger vessel, such as a Romertopf®, if you want to double the recipe, and of course this recipe can also be adapted for chicken.

Pheasant in a Brick

5 small sprigs of thyme

2 cloves garlic, *1 crushed, 1 sliced*

1 pheasant

peel and juice of ½ orange

3–4 slices smoked pancetta (optional)

½ tablespoon olive oil

lots of freshly ground black pepper

Bread Sauce (optional)

3 thick slices bread

⅔ cup water

½ onion, sliced

1 garlic clove, *crushed*

1 bay leaf

3 cloves

1 tablespoon butter, *melted*

3–4 tablespoons double cream

salt and freshly ground black pepper

serves 2

Place a sprig of thyme and a crushed garlic clove inside the pheasant. Tuck sprigs of thyme and slivers of garlic between the legs and the body and the wings and the body. Drape a curl of orange peel over the breast. Wrap the breast in slices of pancetta and place in a soaked chicken brick. Brush with the olive oil, pour over the orange juice, sprinkle with pepper, and place in a cold oven. Turn the oven to 400°F and cook for about 1½ hours or until tender.

Meanwhile, to make the bread sauce, if using, put the bread in a food processor and process to crumbs. Put the water, onion, garlic, bay leaf, and cloves in a pan. Bring to a boil, then set aside to develop the flavors until just before you are ready to serve.

At that point, reheat the water and strain over the breadcrumbs. Add the melted butter and stir in the cream. Season to taste. Add more cream if the sauce is very stiff.

Serve the pheasant with your choice of vegetables, the bread sauce, if using, and a crisp green salad.

A wonderful recipe that can also be used for other meats like pork, veal, or beef. Cook it the day before you want to serve it, remove the meat and flavorings and strain the stock. Chill, defat, and reheat gently before serving.

Garlic Lamb Shanks
with Rosemary

Heat the oil in a skillet, add the lamb shanks and sauté until browned on all sides. Remove from the skillet and add the onions. Cook until softened and translucent, then add the garlic and cook for 2 minutes more. Stir in the carrots, bay leaves, rosemary, and tomatoes. Place the shanks in a soaked Romertopf® or other clay pot so they fit very closely. Add the contents of the skillet, then beef stock to cover.

Place in a cold oven, turn to 450°F until the liquid comes to a boil, reduce to 350°F and simmer for 1–2 hours until the meat is very tender (the time will depend on the size of the shanks).

Chill overnight, skim off the fat and discard, together with the carrots and herbs.

Reduce the stock if necessary to about 2 cups, then reheat the meat in the stock. Serve on a bed of Puy lentils with char-grilled onions.

2 tablespoons olive oil

4 large or 8 small lamb shanks

3 red onions, *sliced*

6 garlic cloves, *crushed*

3 large carrots, *cut into thick chunks*

2 fresh bay leaves

3 sprigs of rosemary

6 large ripe fresh tomatoes, *skinned, quartered, and seeded, or about 1 lb. canned Italian plum tomatoes*

about 2½ cups beef stock (see method)

salt and freshly ground black pepper

To Serve

cooked brown lentils, preferably Puy

char-grilled onions

serves 4

Meat

Salt beef is one of the great Jewish dishes—and it's equally good made with lamb. You'll have to ask your butcher to salt a shoulder or leg of lamb (and he'll be amazed—he'll never have heard of such a thing!). If you don't have a friendly butcher, substitute salt beef or salt pork.

Salt Lamb with Papaya Chili Salsa

1 shoulder or leg of lamb, *salted by the butcher – or salt beef or salt pork*

2 onions, *stuck with 2–4 cloves each*

4 carrots, *thickly sliced diagonally*

2 celery stalks, *coarsely chopped*

2 fresh bay leaves

2 strong stalks of parsley, *crushed with a fork*

1 large sprig of rosemary

2 sprigs of thyme

1 curl of orange peel

6 garlic cloves, or to taste, *crushed*

Papaya Chili Salsa

1 fresh papaya, about 8 oz.

2 sweet bell peppers, 1 red, 1 yellow

1 red chili, *cored, seeded, and diced*

1 tablespoon grated fresh ginger

6 baby gherkins, *finely sliced*

6 tablespoons torn fresh cilantro leaves

zest and juice of 3 limes

sea salt and freshly ground black pepper

serves 4–6

Place the meat in a pan on top of the stove, cover with cold water, and bring slowly to a boil. Remove, rinse, and place in a soaked Romertopf® or glazed clay pot. Surround with the vegetables, herbs, orange peel, and garlic. Add water to cover.

Place in a cold oven, turn to 450°F until the liquid comes to a boil, then reduce the heat and simmer gently for about 2–3 hours or until the meat is melting and tender. Remove the lamb to a serving platter, drizzle with some of the cooking stock, cover, and set aside in a warm place. Strain some of the cooking stock into a small pitcher and reserve. Discard the herbs, garlic, and vegetables.

To make the salsa, peel, seed, and dice the papaya and put in a bowl. Peel the peppers with a vegetable peeler, core, seed, and dice. Add to the bowl with the diced chili, ginger, and gherkins. Stir in the cilantro, lime juice, and zest, and set aside to develop the flavors.

Carve the lamb, drizzle with a little of the cooking stock, then serve hot with the spicy, cold salsa and a few salad leaves.

Note: leftover meat from this recipe makes spectacular sandwiches.

Red-cooking is one of the great cooking methods of Chinese cuisine—meat or poultry is braised in a highly-flavored stock of soy sauce, rice wine, five-spice, and other aromatics. Pork is a favorite Chinese meat, but you could substitute others. Use all light soy sauce, or half light and half dark for stronger flavor. The Chinese tradition is to use five-spice powder and star anise, but some people don't like the taste of anise, and I have sometimes substituted Thai seven-spice—which is delicious too. Chinese cooks strain the cooking stock, freeze it, and use it again and again. The stock becomes more and more flavorful each time it is used.

Chinese
Red-cooked Pork

about 2 lbs. pork roast, such as spareribs, in one whole piece

1 tablespoon Chinese 5-spice or Thai 7-spice

2 cups Chinese rice wine

3 cups chicken stock

2 cups soy sauce

2 tablespoons sugar

10 garlic cloves, *crushed*

2 tablespoons rice vinegar

2 cinnamon sticks

1½-inch piece of fresh root ginger, *sliced*

2 star anise (optional)

2 pieces dried tangerine peel (optional)

6 scallions, *sliced*

serves 4

Rinse the pork in cold running water and pat dry with paper towels. Sprinkle with 5-spice or 7-spice and rub in well.

Pour the rice wine, chicken stock, soy sauce, sugar, garlic, and rice vinegar into a saucepan with the cinnamon sticks and fresh ginger, as well as the star anise and tangerine peel, if using, bring to a boil and simmer for a few minutes to develop the flavors.

Place the pork in a Chinese sand pot or other glazed clay pot, add the sliced scallions, and pour in the flavored stock.

Cook at 450°F until the liquid returns to a boil, then reduce to 300–325°F and simmer for 2–3 hours (the time depends on the size and shape of the joint).

When ready to serve, slice the pork and serve with rice noodles or other Chinese dishes. Alternatively, serve it with European-style mashed potatoes, drizzled with a little of the cooking stock.

An American journalist friend tells me that a good choucroute needs gin to make it really interesting—his grandmother, who grew up in Alsace, the home of choucroute, swore by it! During the long, slow cooking, all the alcohol evaporates, leaving the lovely lemony taste of juniper. (Add extra crushed juniper berries to make sure!) Like many slow-cooked meat dishes, this recipe is even healthier and tastes better if the meat is cooled, chilled (preferably overnight), and defatted before adding the sauerkraut.

Alsacienne

Pork Choucroute

8 thick pork spareribs or 4 thick pork chops

white wine, such as riesling (see method)

2 fresh bay leaves

2 sprigs of sage

2 onions, *finely sliced*

1 carrot, *quartered lengthwise*

6 garlic cloves, *crushed*

1 tablespoon juniper berries, *crushed*

½ cup light stock (chicken or veal)

1 cup gin

salt and freshly ground black pepper

1 lb. jar prepared sauerkraut, *well rinsed under cold running water*sprigs of watercress, to serve

serves 4

Put the pork in a bowl, cover with white wine, add the herbs, onions, carrot, garlic, juniper berries, stock, and gin. Cover and marinate in the refrigerator for about 2 hours or overnight. Transfer to a glazed clay pot. Put the pot in a cold oven and turn to 400°F until the liquid comes to a boil. Reduce to a simmer and cook for 1 hour. Remove the meat, then strain the cooking stock, chill, and skim off the fat.

Place a layer of meat in the bottom of the pot, season, then add a layer of sauerkraut. Repeat until all the meat and sauerkraut is used up. Add the skimmed stock, put into the oven, and heat to boiling point. Reduce the heat to 300–325°F and simmer slowly for 1½–2 hours.

To serve, place 1–2 tablespoons sauerkraut on heated dinner plates and put 2 slices of pork on top. Garnish with watercress, drizzle with the stock, and serve with new potatoes and good cold beer or white wine.

Note: This recipe is also great without the sauerkraut. Simmer the meat for about 1½–2 hours in total, then serve with mustard-mashed potatoes.

This great Italian classic made with veal shanks is just perfect for clay pot cooking. The trick is to cook it long and slow at a low temperature. Take care when serving so the delicious marrow doesn't fall out of the bones—many cooks tie up the meat pieces with string to keep it in. In fact, I must admit that I think the whole point of osso bucco is the marrow and I always choose small pieces of meat, so the ratio of meat to bone and marrow is better. This recipe can also be used with whole lamb shanks. Serve with parsleyed mashed potatoes or pasta tossed in parsley and olive oil.

Osso Bucco

3 tablespoons olive oil

6 onions, *sliced*

4 large or 8 small slices osso bucco (veal shank), *dusted with seasoned flour*

6 garlic cloves, *crushed*

14 oz. canned Italian tomatoes

1 celery stalk, *finely chopped*

a handful of fresh oregano leaves, *chopped*

1 cup red wine

veal or chicken stock, to cover

salt and freshly ground black pepper

Gremolata

3 tablespoons chopped fresh parsley

1 garlic clove, *very finely chopped*

1 tablespoon grated lemon zest

serves 4

Heat the olive oil in a skillet, add the onions, sprinkle with salt, and cook gently until softened and translucent, then transfer to a soaked Romertopf® or glazed clay pot. Add the meat to the skillet, in 2 stages if necessary, brown on all sides, then transfer to the pot.

Add the garlic to the skillet, sauté until golden, then add the canned tomatoes (or fresh and skinned if you have very ripe sweet ones available). Add the celery and oregano, then transfer to the pot.

Deglaze the skillet with the red wine, boil hard for 2 minutes, then pour into the pot. Add veal or chicken stock to cover and place in a cold oven. Turn to 400°F for 30 minutes or until boiling, then reduce to a simmer and cook for 2–3 hours, or until melt-in-your-mouth tender.

To make the gremolata, mix the ingredients together—in a food processor if you like. Serve the osso bucco sprinkled with gremolata.

Jamaicans love chilies—especially their blazingly hot Scotch bonnet (like the habanero chili). Pierce it with a toothpick, then cook it whole in soups or stews and remove before serving (don't break it, or the stew will blow your head off!). A Jamaican friend substitutes a milder hot pepper sauce if she's cooking this for her children.

Caribbean Chili Beef

1 yellow bell pepper, *cored and quartered*

3 large red onions, *sliced into wedges*

3 tablespoons corn or sunflower oil

6 garlic cloves, *crushed*

3 tablespoons flour

1 tablespoon paprika

salt and 1 tablespoon cracked black pepper

1 tablespoon chopped fresh oregano leaves, plus extra, to garnish

3 lbs. beef or lamb, *cut into 1½-inch cubes*

2 tablespoons brown sugar

1 cup dark rum

3 bay leaves

½ teaspoon grated mace or nutmeg

1 tablespoon lime or lemon juice

1 celery stalk, *finely chopped*

2 lbs. ripe tomatoes, *skinned and chopped*

water or stock (see method)

1 large, very hot red chili, *pierced*

serves 4–6

Broil the bell pepper, skin-side up, until the skin is blistered. Scrape off and discard the blackened skin, dice the flesh, and set aside.

Separate the onion wedges into "petals" if preferred, then heat the oil in a skillet, add the onions, and cook until golden. Add the garlic and cook for 2 minutes more. Transfer to a glazed clay pot.

Mix the flour with the paprika, salt, pepper, and chopped oregano leaves, and use it to dust the meat. Add the meat to the skillet in batches, sauté until browned, then transfer to the clay pot.

Add the sugar to the skillet and cook until very dark and caramelized. Deglaze the skillet with the rum, then simmer until reduced to about 2 tablespoons. Add the bay leaves, mace or nutmeg, lime or lemon juice, celery, tomatoes, and sliced broiled pepper. Transfer to the clay pot, add water or stock to cover, and add the whole Jamaican Scotch bonnet chili (or habanero chili).

Cook at 400°F until boiling, then reduce to 300–325°F and simmer gently for 3 hours.

Remove from the oven, discard the chili, sprinkle the beef with sprigs of oregano, and serve with fragrant basmati rice.

One of those warming traditional dishes from what the French call *cuisine grandmère*—but with a modern update of porcini mushrooms. Their rich, smoky flavor puts the finishing touches to a dish that was already perfect! You should always chill the finished dish overnight, remove and discard any fat that rises to the surface, then reheat thoroughly before serving.

Braised Beef with Porcini Mushrooms

Heat half the oil in a skillet, add the sliced onions and sauté until softened and translucent. Transfer to a glazed casserole dish. Brown the carrots and parsnips and add to the pot. Brown the meat in the skillet, then add to the pot. Pour in boiling stock to cover, add the bouquet garni, cover with a lid, and put in a cold oven.

Turn to 450°F and cook until boiling. Reduce to a simmer and cook for 3–4 hours until the meat is falling off the bone.

Remove the meat with a slotted spoon, cool, cover, and chill. Pour the contents of the pot through a strainer and discard the solids. Cool and chill the stock. Discard the fat that rises to the surface.

Next day, soak the porcini in 2 cups boiling water for 30 minutes. Rinse the mushrooms and strain the soaking liquid through filter paper or cheesecloth. Heat the remaining oil in a skillet, add the baby vegetables and sauté gently for 10–15 minutes until the onions are golden.

Return the meat to the clean pot, add the defatted stock and mushroom water, and arrange the baby vegetables and mushrooms over the top. Reheat thoroughly until the baby vegetables are just cooked, then serve.

6 tablespoons olive oil

6 onions, *sliced*

3 large carrots, *cut into 1-inch chunks*

3 parsnips, *cut into 1-inch chunks*

about 3 lbs. beef short ribs or shank, *cut in 3-inch cubes, dusted with seasoned flour*

boiling beef stock (see method)

1 fresh bouquet garni, including 2 fresh bay leaves

1 oz. dried porcini mushrooms

8 baby carrots

8 baby turnips

8 baby parsnips

24 baby onions

salt and freshly ground black pepper

creamy mashed potatoes, *with 2 tablespoons Dijon mustard stirred through,* to serve

serves 4–6

A *tian* is a shallow clay pot in Provençal dialect—and also any dish cooked and served in it. You can be creative with the ingredients and vary them according to your own taste, what's new and fresh at the market, and whether you want to serve this dish as an appetizer or as a vegetable accompaniment to meat or poultry.

Provençal Vegetable Tian

Put the tomatoes in a roasting pan, cut side up, and push slivers of garlic into each. Roast in a preheated oven at 400°F for 30 minutes to remove some of the moisture. Sprinkle the eggplants and zucchinis with salt, and set aside for 30 minutes to extract the moisture. Rinse and pat dry.

Heat half the oil in a large skillet, add the onions, and sauté until softened and translucent. Spread over the base of the *tian*. Arrange the other vegetables on top, in overlapping layers. Sprinkle with salt and pepper.

To make the gremolata, if using, chop the parsley, garlic, and lemon zest together, then mix with the breadcrumbs and 2 tablespoons of the Parmesan. Sprinkle over the top of the *tian*, then cover with the remaining Parmesan. Drizzle with the remaining olive oil and cook at 400°F for about 30–40 minutes or until browned.

6 large ripe red tomatoes, *halved*

4 garlic cloves, *finely sliced*

2 large eggplants, *thickly sliced*

3 yellow zucchinis, *thickly sliced*

6 tablespoons olive oil

2 large onions, *thickly sliced*

salt and freshly ground black pepper

Gremolata *(optional)*

4 tablespoons chopped fresh flat-leaf parsley

6 garlic cloves, *crushed*

grated zest of 2 lemons

about ½ cup dried breadcrumbs

6 tablespoons grated Parmesan cheese

serves 6

Tagines are the conical terra cotta cooking pots of Morocco, and also the dishes cooked in them. Use a tagine or any lidded clay pot for this modern version of the classic *Couscous aux Sept Légumes*.

Moroccan
Chickpea Tagine
with Spring Vegetables

1½ cups dried chickpeas (garbanzo beans)

2 tablespoons olive oil

2 onions, *sliced*

1–6 garlic cloves (to taste), *crushed*

1 teaspoon cumin seeds

1 teaspoon crushed coriander seeds

1 cinnamon stick

2½ cups easy-cook couscous

3 cups boiling vegetable or chicken stock

2 tablespoons harissa paste

4–8 baby new potatoes, *unpeeled*

½ cup diced pumpkin

½ cup diced orange sweet potatoes

4–8 baby carrots

4–8 baby zucchinis, green and yellow

4 baby pattypan squash, *halved*

½ cup small French beans

½ cup snow peas

salt and freshly ground black pepper

serves 4

Soak the chickpeas overnight in cold water to cover. Drain. Heat the olive oil in a skillet and sauté the onions until soft. Add the garlic, cumin, coriander seeds, and cinnamon. Cook for 1 minute, add the chickpeas and cook for 1 more minute. Transfer to a soaked bean pot or tagine, cover with water, put on the lid, and place in a cold oven. Turn to 400°F until the liquid boils. Reduce to a simmer and cook for 2 hours or until the chickpeas are soft (the time will depend on the age of the chickpeas).

Place the couscous in a heatproof bowl, pour over the boiling stock, stir in the harissa paste, and set aside to keep warm.

Add the potatoes to the pot, season with salt and pepper, return to a boil and cook for 10 minutes. Add the pumpkin, sweet potato, and carrots and cook for 10 minutes more. Add the zucchinis, pattypans, and beans, cook for 5 minutes, then add the snow peas, replace the lid, and serve immediately. Drain the couscous if necessary, spoon on to a serving plate, and top with the chickpea tagine.

Note: Chickpeas and other dried peas and beans are perfect for clay pot cooking. Soak them overnight, bring them to a boil, then reduce the heat and simmer until tender. Red kidney beans must be boiled hard first on top of the stove for at least 15 minutes to destroy toxins.

I can't tell you how delicious this recipe is—and simple! You can also peel the onions and cook with chicken pieces in a tian.

Oven-roasted Onions
with
Anchovies

4 onions, *unpeeled, halved lengthwise*

8–16 small anchovy fillets

sea salt

serves 4

Using a teaspoon or a small knife, pry out the middle petals from each onion half, leaving a small indentation. Stuff 1–2 anchovy fillets into each hollow, place the onions in an onion baker, tagine, casserole, or tian, and sprinkle with salt to help them soften quicker. Place in a cold oven, turn to 400°F, and cook for 40 minutes or until tender. If using a lidded vessel, remove the lid, and continue cooking until the edges of the onions are golden brown. Press the onions out of their skins and serve beside roast meat or on top of risotto.

Spiced Chickpeas

1½ cups dried chickpeas, *soaked overnight*

1 tablespoon vegetable oil

1 tablespoon fresh ginger purée

1 tablespoon fresh garlic purée

1 tablespoon ajwain (optional)

1 teaspoon red chili powder

1 teaspoon ground turmeric

½ cup plain yogurt

3 tablespoons heavy cream

2 tablespoons lime juice

sea salt

serves 4

Drain the chickpeas and place in a bean pot or casserole with cold water to cover. Place in a cold oven, turn to 400°F and bring to a boil. Reduce to 300°F and simmer for about 2 hours, or until done (the time depends on the age of the chickpeas). Drain, sprinkle with salt and place in a heated bowl.

Heat the oil in a skillet, add the ginger, garlic, ajwain, if using, chili powder, and turmeric and stir-fry for about 1 minute until the garlic is lightly golden. Stir in the yogurt and cream and heat gently without boiling. Stir in the lime juice; pour the mixture over the chickpeas and toss well. Serve hot or cold.

A delicious version of the classic Tuscan dish of potatoes fried with garlic and rosemary.

Oven-baked Potatoes
with Sage and Garlic

Heat the olive oil in a skillet and sauté the garlic until lightly browned. Place the potatoes in a potato pot, cover with the oil and garlic, add sprigs of sage, bay leaves, and sea salt, then cover with the lid. Place in a cold oven, turn to 400°F and cook for 1 hour, or until the potatoes are done (the time will depend on their size and the speed of your oven).

3 tablespoons olive oil

6 garlic cloves, *crushed*

1 lb. new potatoes

3 sprigs of sage

3 fresh bay leaves

sea salt

serves 4

Baked sweet potatoes with spicy butter are great as a vegetarian dish, or as an accompaniment to meat or poultry for the rest of us!

Thai Sweet Potatoes

4 orange-fleshed sweet potatoes

2 tablespoons grated kaffir lime zest

1 teaspoon garlic purée

2 tablespoons ginger purée

4–6 tablespoons softened butter

sea salt

serves 4

Prick the sweet potatoes 1–2 times each and place in a potato baker or clay dish. Brush with melted butter, put in a cold oven, turn to 400°F and cook for about 30 minutes, or until tender.

Mix the lime zest, garlic, and ginger in a small bowl with 1 tablespoon butter. Make a slit in each sweet potato and spoon in the mixture. Return to the oven for 5 minutes, then serve.

I think I like these tropical variations of *tarte tatin* made with mango or pineapple better than the traditional pear or apple versions. The contrast between the sweet sauce, feathery puff pastry, and the perfect fruit—especially the slightly sour pineapple—is just delicious. We grew mangoes and pineapples on the farm where I grew up, and my mother created dozens of wonderful ways to cook with them. This is one.

Mango Tarte Tatin

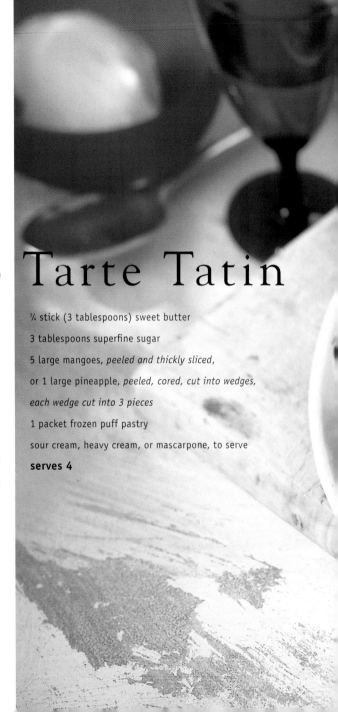

Melt the butter in a skillet, add the sugar and cook, stirring, until the mixture turns golden brown. Stir in the mango or pineapple pieces until well covered with the mixture. Spoon into an ovenproof china pie dish.

Roll out the pastry and place on top of the filling, crimping the edges so they lie inside the edges of the dish, then cut a few steam holes in the top of the pastry. Cook in a preheated oven at 400°F for about 15 minutes until the pastry is golden and puffy. Loosen the crust, place a plate over the top, invert, remove the plate, and serve with cream.

¼ stick (3 tablespoons) sweet butter

3 tablespoons superfine sugar

5 large mangoes, *peeled and thickly sliced,* or 1 large pineapple, *peeled, cored, cut into wedges, each wedge cut into 3 pieces*

1 packet frozen puff pastry

sour cream, heavy cream, or mascarpone, to serve

serves 4

Desserts

Rhubarb and Quince Crumble

Quinces are beautiful fruit, related to the apple and pear. Slice them into a bowl of water with lemon juice to keep them from browning. If you can't find quinces (they're in season in late autumn), use apples instead. This dessert is pretty and pink—quince, which must always be eaten cooked, turns pink in the heat. I like this served with sour cream or cream.

Place the rhubarb, quince, and ginger in an ovenproof china pie dish and sprinkle with sugar. Put the topping ingredients in a food processor and process briefly to fine crumbs. Spread the crumble mixture over the top and cook at 400°F for about 40 minutes. The fruit sauce will bubble up through the pale crumbly topping.

1 lb. young rhubarb, *cut into chunks*

1 lb. quinces, *peeled and sliced*

4 pieces stem ginger in syrup, *finely sliced*

6 tablespoons superfine sugar

Crumble Topping

2 tablespoons superfine sugar

6 tablespoons all-purpose flour

4 tablespoons sweet butter

serves 4

Bread and Butter Pudding

Up-market chefs have fiddled about with this traditional English pudding, using brioche, apricot sandwiches, or panettone instead of the bread. All these variations are marvelous, but I prefer it plain or with raisin bread (and fresh ginger purée because I adore ginger!)

Mix the butter and ginger, if using, then spread over the bread. Place the slices, crusts upward, in a large, buttered ovenproof china pie dish. Sprinkle with golden raisins and sugar. Beat the eggs and milk together, pour over the bread, and soak for 5 minutes. Bake for 35–40 minutes at 350°F or until the bread is fluffy, the custard set, and the top browned. Dust with confectioners' sugar and serve with a pitcher of cream.

½ stick (4 tablespoons) softened sweet butter, *for spreading*

1 tablespoon ginger purée (optional)

6 slices good white bread, *preferably Italian (thickly cut)*

2 tablespoons golden raisins

3 tablespoons superfine sugar

2 eggs, lightly beaten

2¾ cups milk

confectioners' sugar, *for dusting*

serves 4